Christmas List Book

Designed by Roni Akmon

We would like to thank the following for their permission
to reproduce certain illustrations in this book:
Fine Art Photographs, Bridgeman Art Library, and Picturepoint Library.

Efforts have been made to find the copyright holders of material used in this
publication. We apologize for any omissions or errors and will be pleased to
include the appropriate acknowledgements in future editions.

ISBN 1-884807-07-0

Published by Blushing Rose Publishing
P.O. Box 2238
San Anselmo, CA 94979

Printed and bound in Singapore

Christmas List Book

To: *Lisa & Andy*

From: *Jim & Claudene*

Date: *12-94*

Designed by Roni Akmon
Written by Nancy Cogan Akmon

Blushing Rose Publishing
San Anselmo, California

Christmas

Christmas comes but
once a year,
and when it comes
it brings good cheer.

A MERRY CHRISTMAS

Christmas Cards

We seem too busy every day to say the things
we want to say;
Our deepest thoughts we seem to hide until we reach
the Christmas tide. 'Tis then we send to friends again,
In happy words the old refrain—'Very Merry Christmas'

—*Verse from a Victorian Christmas Card*

Christmas Card List

Christmas Card List

_____

_____

_____

_____

_____

_____

_____

_____

_____

_____

Christmas Card List

Christmas Card List

Christmas Card List

Christmas Card List

Christmas Card List

Christmas Card List

Christmas Card List

Christmas Card List

Christmas Card List

Christmas Presents

What can I give Him, Poor as I am?
If I were a sheperd, I would give him a lamb;
If I were a Wise Man, I would do my part—
But what I can give Him, I Give my heart.

—Christina Rossetti

Christmas Presents List

Christmas Presents List

Christmas Presents List

Christmas Presents List

_____

_____

_____

_____

_____

_____

_____

_____

_____

_____

Christmas Presents List

Christmas Presents List

Christmas Presents List

Christmas Presents List

Christmas Presents List

Christmas Presents List

Christmas Presents List

Christmas Presents List

Christmas Presents List

Christmas Menus

Christmas is coming, the Goose is getting Fat,
Please put a penny in the old man's hat.
If you haven't got a penny, a ha'penny will do,
If you haven't got a ha'penny—God bless you!

—a traditional Children's Rhyme

Christmas Menus

Christmas Menus

_____

_____

_____

_____

_____

_____

_____

_____

_____

_____

Christmas Menus

Christmas Menus

Christmas Menus

Christmas Menus

Christmas Menus

Christmas Menus

_____

_____

_____

_____

_____

_____

_____

_____

_____

Christmas Menus

_____

_____

_____

_____

_____

_____

_____

_____

_____

_____

ILLUSTRATED LONDON NEWS

Wishing you a Happy CHRISTMAS

CHRISTMAS 1895

WISHING YOU A   HAPPY NEW YEAR

Holiday Party

When as you sing at Christmas...
And welcome in the brigh...
And feast and laugh and dance and...
And open gifts on Christmas day
Pause as you hear the angels' word
And don't neglect the little birds...

Anonymous, 1909

Holiday Parties

_____

_____

_____

_____

_____

_____

_____

_____

_____

_____

Holiday Parties

Holiday Parties

Holiday Parties

Holiday Parties

_____

_____

_____

_____

_____

_____

_____

_____

_____

Holiday Parties

_____

_____

_____

_____

_____

_____

_____

_____

_____

_____

Holiday Parties

Holiday Parties

_____

_____

_____

_____

_____

_____

_____

_____

_____

Holiday Parties

Holiday Events

But give me holly, Bold and jolly,
Honest, prickly, Shining holly,
Pluck me holly, Leaf and berry
For the day when I make merry.

—Christina Rossetti

Holiday Events

_____

_____

_____

_____

_____

_____

_____

_____

_____

Holiday Events

_____

_____

_____

_____

_____

_____

_____

_____

_____

Holiday Events

Holiday Events

Holiday Events

_____

_____

_____

_____

_____

_____

_____

_____

_____

_____

Holiday Events

Holiday Events

_____

_____

_____

_____

_____

_____

_____

_____

_____

_____

Holiday Events

Holiday Events

_____

_____

_____

_____

_____

_____

_____

_____

_____

_____

Holiday Events

Holiday Events

Holiday Guests

ith Holly and Ivy so green and so gay,
We deck up our houses as fresh as the day,
With bay and rosemary and laurel complete,
and everyone now Is a King in conceit.

—Anonymous, 17th Century

Holiday Guest List

Holiday Guest List

Holiday Guest List

Holiday Guest List

Holiday Guest List

Holiday Guest List

Holiday Guest List

Holiday Guest List

A Blessing

od Bless the master of this house,
The mistress also,
And all the little children
That round the table go:

And all your kin and kinsfolk,
That dwell both far and near;
I wish you a merry Christmas
and a Happy New Year.

—Anonymous, 17th Century